Bless the Lord

by
Graham Jeffery

Kevin Mayhew

KEVIN MAYHEW LTD
Rattlesden Bury St Edmunds
Suffolk England
IP30 0SZ

ISBN 0 86209 449 6

Printed in Great Britain

You are wonderful
to me, Lord.

You made
my mother and father,

my teddy
and all my toys.

You made Tibby
and the old lady next door.

home
MILK

You made everyone
in our street.

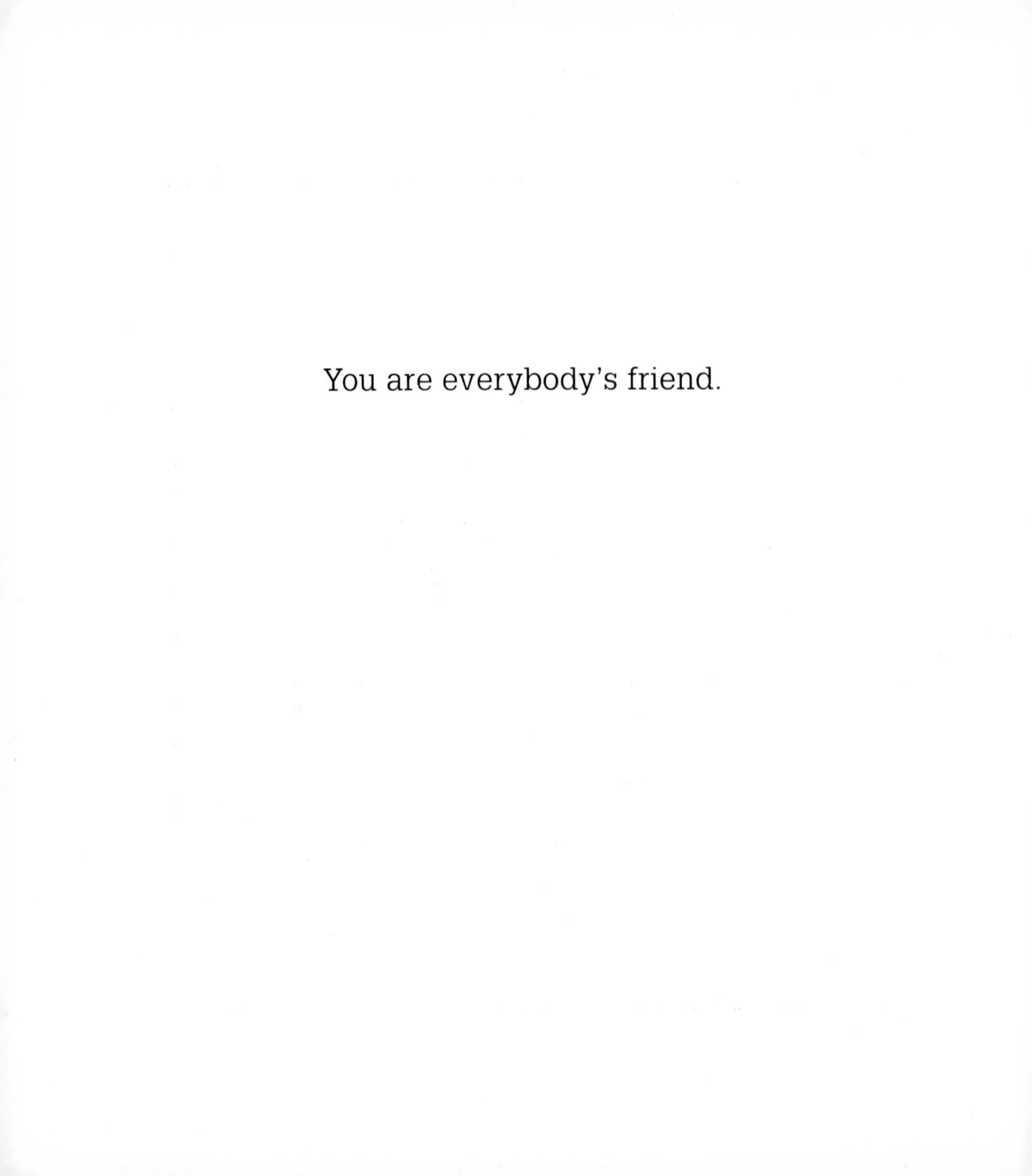

You are everybody's friend.

LIBRARY

You made the sun and rain,

the moon and the stars.

You made trees and flowers,

and all the animals –

elephants and foxes,

horses and cows,

pigs and chickens,

FOOD

frogs and fish,

and birds that fly in the sky.

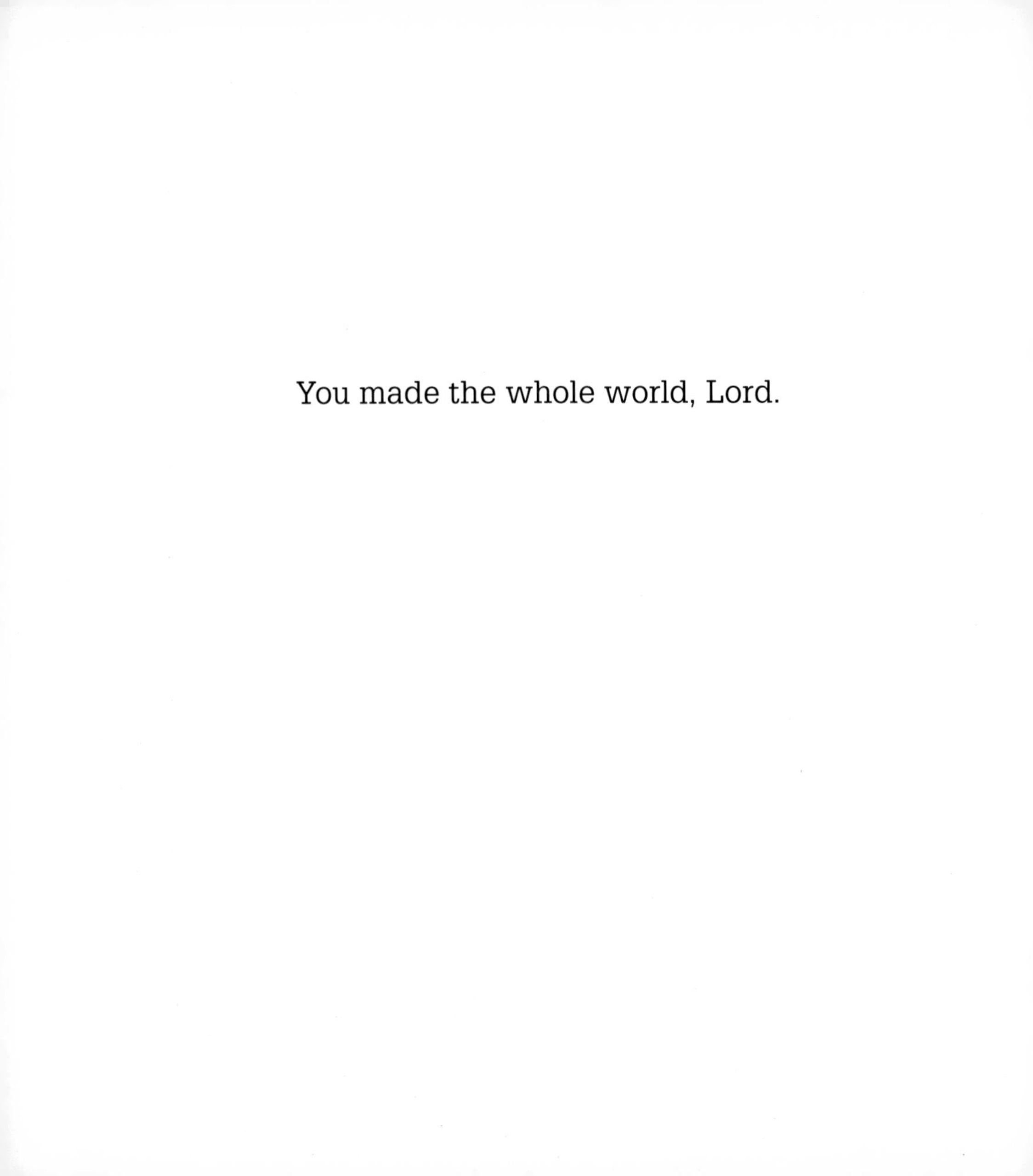

You made the whole world, Lord.

And I want everything
to love you, too.

Woof
Meow

Amen.